W9-BMK-066

THE HYDRA

MONSTERS OF MYTHOLOGY

25 VOLUMES

Hellenic

Amycus
Anteus
The Calydonian Boar
Cerberus
Chimaera
The Cyclopes
The Dragon of Boeotia
The Furies
Geryon
Harpalyce
Hecate
The Hydra
Ladon
Medusa
The Minotaur
The Nemean Lion
Procrustes
Scylla and Charybdis
The Sirens
The Spear-birds
The Sphinx

Norse

Fafnir
Fenris

Celtic

Drabne of Dole
Pig's Ploughman

MONSTERS OF MYTHOLOGY

THE HYDRA

Bernard Evslin

CHELSEA HOUSE PUBLISHERS

New York   Philadelphia

— 1989 —

EDITOR
Remmel Nunn

ART DIRECTOR
Maria Epes

PICTURE RESEARCHER
Susan Quist

SENIOR DESIGNER
Victorià Tomaselli

EDITORIAL ASSISTANTS
Heather Lewis, Mark Rifkin

5 7 9 8 6

Library of Congress Cataloging-in-Publication Data

Evslin, Bernard.
The Hydra.

(Monsters of mythology)
Summary: Recounts the myth of the hundred-headed
creature which was slain by the hero Hercules.
1. Hydra (Greek mythology)—Juvenile literature.
2. Heracles (Greek mythology)—Juvenile literature.
3. Iole (Greek mythology)—Juvenile literature.
[1. Hydra (Greek mythology) 2. Hercules (Greek
mythology) 3. Mythology, Greek] I. Title. II. Series:
Evslin, Bernard. Monsters of mythology.
BL820.H93E95   1989   398.2′1   88-20248

ISBN 1-55546-253-7

Printed and bound in Mexico.

In one version of this tale, it was not Hercules but
the heroic physician, Asclepius, who fought the
monster and cut off its hundred poison heads—
which immediately turned into a hundred streams
of pure healing waters. And this, in turn, led to a
whole theory of pharmacology. In the spirit of that
earlier legend, I dedicate this book to
BILL EVSLIN
wonderful son and superb doctor

Contents

Characters

Gods

Zeus (ZOOS)	King of the Gods
Hera (HEE ruh)	Zeus's wife, Queen of the Gods
Hermes (HUR meez)	Zeus's son, the Messenger God
Hecate (HECK uh tee)	Queen of the Harpies
Iris (EYE rihs)	Rainbow Goddess, messenger to Hera

Titans

Boreas (BOH re ahs)	The North Wind
Eurus (YOO ruhs)	The East Wind

Notus (NOH tuhs)	The South Wind
Zephyrus (ZEF ehr uhs)	The West Wind

Mortals

Hercules (HER ku leez)	Strongest man in the world
Iole (EYE oh lee)	Daughter of Iris, a very determined girl
Eurystheus (yoo RISS thee uhs)	King of Mycenae, Hercules' taskmaster
Copreus (COH pre uhs)	Doer of dirty jobs for Eurystheus

Monsters

The Hydra (HY druh)	A hundred-headed reptile, extremely lethal
Cancer	A giant crab

Others

Meadow Nymphs

Frost Demons

Arctic Wolves

Arctic Owls

Polar Bears

A Flock of Tiny Tailors

1

War of the Winds

ong ago, when the world was very new, the silver-eyed Titan, Astraeus, trysted in a corner of the sky with Eos, the dawn goddess, siring the Four Winds and a litter of stars.

The Wind Titans quartered the earth, each dwelling in his own castle—Notus in an ivory pile on the southern edge of things; Eurus in a jade palace on the eastern edge; kindly Zephyrus in an oaken tower on the western rim, while brutal, blustering Boreas dwelt in the north in a castle whose beams were walrus tusk and mammoth bone, whose walls were solid blocks of ice.

Boreas slept through the summer and awoke in early autumn, raging with hunger and evil tempered, ready to howl across the sky, bending trees and breaking ships, toppling hillside villages into the valleys below, and sweeping coastal villages into the sea.

Eurus, the East Wind, was of a less violent nature than Boreas but could be deadly in his own way, striking suddenly out of fair skies. He was a menace to shipping when his mood was foul, and was much feared by mariners. He was especially cruel and capricious in the springtime, and seamen then were careful to keep lee shore to the eastward. At other times he would hover over swampland, drawing in great breaths of pestilential air and letting them out in malarial gusts so that people sickened and died.

Notus was also treacherous. At times he would blow warmly out of the south, scattering clouds and drying the fields. Often, though, he drove cold rain before him, and savage hailstorms that could scythe down a season's crop in a single night.

But the West Wind, Zephyrus, was a friend to man. He came in the spring with warm gentle showers. And the waters of the melting snow and the warm rain sank into the earth and brought up flowers and young trees and all the crops that feed mankind.

The Wind brothers were not sociable. They did not mingle with the other Titans, nor, indeed with any of the god tribe—with one exception.

They passionately followed Iris, the rainbow goddess, who appeared after storms, casting her arch of colors across the new-washed sky. The Winds hovered, watching as she danced on her radiant bow and sang a fair-weather song. For three of the winds had fallen madly in love with her.

But she ignored the tempestuous wooing of Boreas, and the rich gifts of Eurus, and the honeyed words of Notus. She preferred Zephyrus—who loved someone else.

So the Winds went to war.

Eurus and Notus, although rivals for Iris's affections, were quite willing to join forces against Boreas, who was much the strongest of the brothers. Once rid of him, they thought, they would be able to fight it out between themselves on more or less equal terms.

Choosing a time when Boreas was sleeping his summer sleep, the South Wind blew into the arctic wastes, melting the ice floes, making the sea swell into a mighty flood. The East Wind, who had been waiting to strike, now blew at an angle, whipping the swollen seas into a huge torrent that rushed toward the North Wind's castle, threatening to drown him as he slept.

But it was very dangerous to arouse Boreas. Awakened too soon by the roaring of a strange surf, he saw a mass of wind-driven waters cresting toward his castle. Angrier than he had ever been before in his wrathful life, he filled his chest with icy air and blew it out in a blast that froze the waters, forming an ice mountain where there had been a flat stretch of permafrost.

But the stilling of the waters did not quench his fury. He immediately launched a counterattack. Blackening the sky with his cape, he stormed out of the north, hurling gales before him—which grew to hurricane force as their coldness met the warmer

*The North Wind roared over the rain
forests, freezing man and beast. . .*

airs. Leaving a swath of destruction in his wake, Boreas flew farther south than he had ever been—over deserts and jungles. And the people there, and the apes and elephants and lions and zebras, whimpered and shuddered and stared at the sky from which strange white stuff was falling. The terrible cold whiteness lay on the ground like a shroud. Indeed, hordes of those who dwelt in southern lands froze to death.

Then the North Wind turned east. He roared over the rain forests, freezing man and beast, and sheathing the trees in ice so that they glittered and chimed. All the way to the eastern rim of the world Boreas flew, and blew down the wonderful jade palace belonging to Eurus before turning north again.

Eurus and Notus knew when they were beaten. They sent messages of surrender to Boreas, humbly begging his pardon and asking to meet with him so that they might apologize properly. Traveling north in abjectly gentle breezes they visited Boreas in his ice castle, and begged him to grant a truce.

Huge, fur clad, he sat on his walrus-ivory throne, frowning down at them as they stammered out their apologies. In the enormous, freezing throne room, where arctic wolves prowled like hounds and great white arctic owls flew like parakeets, the North Wind sat in state, and his younger brothers trembled before him.

"I shall pardon you on one condition," he growled. "You must promise to abandon all claim to Iris."

"We do! We do!" cried Eurus.

"But," said Notus slyly, "we are not the problem, you know. She looks with favor upon none of us. For some weird reason she seems to prefer Zephyrus."

"Nonsense!" roared Boreas. "Where did you get that idea?"

"I happened to meet a meadow nymph whose clan gathers wildflowers for the colors that Iris flings across the sky. And she told me that all the nymphs are gossiping about this. For when Iris touches earth, she wanders about, murmuring 'Zephyrus . . . Zephyrus . . .' and gazes yearningly westward."

"I'll give those gabby sluts something else to wag their tongues about," said Boreas. "Iris will be mine before the month is out."

"How will you manage that, noble sir?" asked Notus.

"In my own way, the simple direct North Wind way. I'll snatch her out of the sky and bring her here. And keep her close until she agrees to marry me."

"A brilliant plan," cried Eurus. "Bold and brilliant. Is there any way we can help?"

"I need no help from pitiful puling puffs of nothing like you two. Just skulk back to your own lairs and stay there until I give you permission to leave."

"Thank you, mighty Brother," cried Notus. "May your courtship be prosperous."

"Get out," growled Boreas.

And the South Wind and the East Wind bowed and smirked their way out of the ice castle, vowing to each other never to cross their powerful brother again, no matter what.

2

Young Hercules

At the age of fifteen Hercules was still only half grown, but bigger than most men, and much stronger. He had stopped wrestling with other boys because he was afraid of hurting them. Yet, he knew, he had to find some way of using the perilous strength he had been given. At times he felt that only the iron hoops of his ribs kept his energy caged, kept it from bursting his keg of a chest and splitting him like an overripe melon.

So he sought ways of spending his energy. He uprooted small trees and wrestled yearling bears. It was at this time that the vengeful North Wind blew too far south, bringing arctic weather to places that had never known real winter before. And when Hercules went out that day to seek bears to wrestle, he found a land transformed by snow. Although his body was almost hairless, his skin was tough as horsehide, and he was untroubled by the cold. In fact, he found the snow helpful. It held animal tracks, among them the imprint of bear paws—and this clear spoor, he knew, would save him hours of searching.

Now he had wrestled all the yearling bears in the Theban forests. They knew him well and enjoyed the wrestling as much as he did, and never used their teeth and claws against him. And now, when Hercules heard a bear growling savagely in the underbrush, he couldn't believe it was growling at him, but that it had been attacked by a lion—the only beast about that would dare attack a bear.

Hercules raced toward the sound to see if he could help. He had run only a few steps, however, when something came charging out of the brush. He stared in amazement. What he saw was a giant wearing armor, and it was growling like an angry bear. Looking more closely, he saw that it *was* a bear rearing up on its hind legs, but such a bear as he had never seen—a full-sized one, sheathed in ice. The sun striking off the ice made it glitter like armor.

It was such a bear as he had never seen—
a full-sized one, sheathed in ice.

It moved toward him, growling more savagely than ever. Now bears do not usually grow angry unless they feel themselves threatened, or, in the case of a female, if she sees someone approaching her cubs. Thinking fast, Hercules realized what must have happened. This bear, emerging from a swim in the lake, had been caught in the sudden frost, and the water froze on its fur, sheathing it in ice. This made the beast very uncomfortable. And now, in confused rage, it sought someone to fix the blame on.

The huge glittering animal was very close now, and Hercules prepared to fight. It was his custom, in a fight, always to charge first. But he hesitated. He did not relish the idea of those arms closing about him in a mighty icy hug. Nor did he particularly want to hurt the bear. But it was coming at him; he had to do something. He cast his spear with the full-armed throw that could split a tree—and was astounded to see it skid off the bear, just chipping away a few flakes of ice. He realized then that the thick ice sheath was indeed like armor, but even better protection because it was slippery.

So Hercules, who had never avoided a fight in his short life, whirled now and raced away.

Denied his wrestling that day, and feeling himself aflame with the unfinished fight, he galloped home through the heavy snow, seeking the thickest drifts to plow through.

The weather warmed again, and spring resumed. The fund of wild energy that was in Hercules seemed to grow and grow. He wandered far from the city and began to climb mountains, the steeper the better, not plodding up, but running as hard as he could, and never stopping to rest.

One day, he came upon a range of foothills, not too high but quite steep, and he happily raced up one slope, over the top, down the back slope, and on to another hill—until he had done every one of the eight hills without stopping.

It was a hot day, and coming down the last hill he was delighted to find that a fast-moving stream was tumbling over a rocky ledge to become a waterfall. Without doffing his tunic, he jumped under the fall and stood under the icy shower, shouting with joy. Cooled off now, he began to explore, and found himself on a high meadow, cupped by the eight hills. It was the loveliest meadow he had ever seen, carpeted by wildflowers, a great mix of them, filling the air with fragrance and the sleepy hum of bees, and blazing with sudden pure colors among thick grass and loose underbrush.

This meadow became young Hercules' secret place, and he came there as often as he could after wrestling bears, and up-rooting trees, and racing up and down the hills. He was further delighted to find that the meadow was inhabited by a clan of flower nymphs, who spent part of each morning plucking the wild blossoms and steeping them in a great vat of springwater. As soon as they saw Hercules, though, they would leave the flowers to steep themselves and run across the meadow to dance with him.

At first, he thought they were making wine in the vat, but when he asked for a drink they laughed at him.

"That is not wine we're making," said a nymph named Numa, "but various dyes. For know, oh handsome youth, that we serve Iris, the rainbow goddess. Every so often she comes down here and dips her gauze into our vat; they become the colored streamers which she flings across the sky after a storm, and which then gather themselves into a great bridge of colors."

"Do you think I might see Iris sometime?" asked Hercules. "Will you tell me when she's about to visit?"

"No, we don't think so," said Numa. "She's enchantingly beautiful. Once you saw her you would fall in love with her and forget all about us."

"Love? Love . . ." said Hercules. "I don't know. I told my mother I thought I was in love with all of you, but she laughed at me and said I was much too young to know what love was."

"Tell her we'll teach you," said the nymph.

When Hercules next came to the meadow, it seemed deserted. He listened for the happy voices of the nymphs, but did not hear them. Then he did hear something. It was not a happy sound. It seemed like the sound of weeping—not an ugly aggressive sobbing, but like the mourning of doves. He searched and found the nymphs huddled in a glade. All were weeping, but each one was trying to comfort the one next to her, while still weeping herself.

"What's the matter?" cried Hercules.

They lifted tear-stained faces to him. Then arose and surrounded him, all talking at once.

"One at a time," said Hercules. "I can't make out what you're saying."

It was the loveliest meadow . . .
blazing with sudden pure colors among
thick grass and loose underbrush

Then Numa gestured the others to silence, and said, "Let me tell him. Remember that rainstorm we had last week? Well, when the air cleared, we watched the sky because we knew that after so hard a rain Iris would appear. And she did. She stretched her bow across the sky, and we rejoiced to see that one foot of it was planted here because that meant she would slide

*An enormous black-caped figure
came hurtling down toward Iris.*

down and visit us. Then we saw her sliding. She grew larger and larger as we watched until we could see the yellow hair whipping about her face, and were calling to her joyously when, suddenly, the sky blackened, blotting the rainbow. An enormous black-caped figure came hurtling down toward Iris. It engulfed her, snatched her off her bridge of colors, took her into its darkness—

spread the wings of its cape and flew north. Oh woe and wail away, our Iris was gone, our lovely goddess. She's gone, gone, gone, and we'll never see her again."

"She's a goddess, after all," said Hercules. "And can escape from whatever monster it was that took her."

"Ah, no," said Numa. "It was no monster but a Titan, a Wind Titan, the most powerful of all. It was Boreas, the North Wind; we recognized him. And from his clutch no one escapes."

"And he flew back north, you say?"

"Yes," she said. "There he dwells in an ice castle on the very northern rim of the earth. And there, no doubt, he means to cage up our poor bright Iris, and freeze her into submission."

"Farewell," said Hercules.

"Where are you going?" cried the nymphs.

"North," he said.

3

The Frost Demons

he fleet, joyful goddess who had used the entire blue vault of heaven as her playground was unprepared for captivity. As soon as she knew the great clutch of the North Wind upon her, when his black cloak quenched her colors, she felt so grossly violated that she wished to shed her immortality and die.

But she was a goddess. She could not die. She could suffer, but not die.

She tried to call for help. The terrible icy clutch froze the screams in her throat and she could utter no sound. Boreas clasped her to him as he flew northward. His cloak covered her body, but her head poked out, and she could watch the water sliding away far below.

She swooned briefly then. When she came to, she saw a whale spouting; its spume froze, glinting in the weak sunlight and casting fractured colors. The shards of light reminded her of her own blotted colors, and a hot pang of grief pierced her breast.

But the heat thawed her. Her courage awoke, and she began to think how she might free herself. "I'm supposed to have many friends," she thought. "Will they dare? Will they attempt to save me? Who among my admirers on Olympus will brave the North

Wind's wrath? Oh, the gods can be courageous where their own interests are concerned, but they don't like to put themselves out for anyone else. There may be someone though. I can only hope there may be one who will follow me here and seek to rescue me. But how will anyone find me? Who could possibly guess that I've been taken to this icy waste? If I could only leave some kind of sign. But of course! There is one unmistakable sign of my presence. How stupid of me not to think of it before."

But she knew she could do nothing yet, so she bided her time. And when Boreas came to earth and began to drag her toward his ice castle, she slipped his grasp and flung her colors into the sky—where they immediately froze.

And that arch of color frozen into the leaden sky was what Hercules saw as he approached the rim of the world. He knew then that he must be nearing the North Wind's castle and pressed forward with renewed hope.

Franz Marc *Blue Horse with Rainbow* (1913)

And that arch of color frozen into the leaden sky was what Hercules saw as he approached the rim of the world.

Now, Boreas knew that he was well hated, and that many enemies wished his destruction. And while he also suspected that they were too much afraid of him to attempt an assault, he did not believe in taking chances and had surrounded himself with creatures so fearsome that no one would dare trespass.

The icy plain about his castle was the hunting ground of great wolves that would attack any stranger. Polar bears also prowled; they would devour anything that moved except their own cubs. Above hovered arctic owls, larger than eagles. Boreas used them like falcons. At his whistle they would stoop upon any living thing passing below, raking with their meat-hook claws, stabbing with their murderous beaks.

Worst of all, though, were the frost demons. They looked like living icicles, but were not made of ice. They were made of translucent metal with a vital thread of pink fire pulsing inside. Stumpy legs propelled their long tapering bodies with terrific speed. After a short run they would launch themselves, traveling through the air faster than any arrow shot from any bow. When their pointed heads hit their targets—tree, wall, beast, or armored man—they would pass right through and come out the other side.

Hercules' first impulse when faced by an enemy was to attack. And at this time he was very young and exceedingly rash. Nevertheless, he realized that this array of beasts and demons was far too formidable for him to make any headlong assault. His only remote chance of any kind of success, he knew, was to make a plan.

First he had to hide himself, for the wolves were already beginning to growl as if they had caught his scent, and the great owls were screaming overhead. Fortunately, the castle grounds were littered with bones and skulls of beasts that had been hunted and eaten. He dived among this rubble of bones, burrowed in and made a nest. From there he could peer out and see what was happening without being seen himself.

He stared in wonder at the enormous polar bears and the gigantic white wolves. He carefully studied the canopy of white owls. Most of all, though, he was impressed by those living weapons, the frost demons. He watched in astonishment as they hunted.

For the frost demons used themselves as augers. One of them would hurl itself into the air and come down headfirst. Its iron-hard pointed skull would drive a hole into the ice. Again and again it would do this, enlarging the hole. When it was large enough, the demon would crouch at its edge and wait there until a walrus poked its head out. Then the demon would seize the walrus by its tusks, flip it out of the water onto the ice, and eat it raw.

After the demons were sated and left their water holes, the polar bears would come and squat in their turn, waiting for walruses.

Watching them, Hercules began to put together a battle plan. It meant utter risk, he knew, but it was his one slim chance.

He waited until the frost demons had left the largest water hole and the polar bears had gathered. Then he burst from his nest of bones, hurtled across the ice, leaped mightily, turned in the air, and dived over the circle of bears—into the hole. He had gulped a great breath of air while diving and held that breath as he entered the water and felt the viselike cold trying to crush his rib cage.

He didn't linger in the water. All he wanted to do was to get wet. Groping with his hands, he found the rim of the hole and pushed down with all the strength of his arms while doing a frog kick with his legs—lifting himself into the air again, soaring the other way over the circle of bears.

The water froze on him before he hit the ground. Now he was encased in ice—just as that bear had been back in Thebes, that bear whose icy armor had stopped his spear.

Two polar bears closed with him. He stood there, legs planted. They couldn't knock him over. They tried to rake him with their claws, tried to crush him in their jaws, but neither fang nor claw could pierce the hard ice. He swung his arms like clubs; they cracked against the bears, smashing skulls. The polar bears fell.

Wolves attacked. They leaped upon this icy form, detecting the meat underneath. They tried to drag him down, savaging him with their teeth. They could not budge him; their fangs could not pierce the ice. He swung his arms again, clubbing the wolves. They dodged away from him and fled, whimpering.

Now the frost demons attacked. On their stumpy legs they whizzed across the ground with terrific speed, launched themselves into the air and came toward him like a flight of living arrows. Pointed heads hit him, seven of them at once, and bore him to the ground. Then the demons leaped, turning in the air, diving down at him, trying to pierce him with their spearlike heads.

Chips of ice flew but the armor held. Hercules scrambled to his feet, grasped two of the demons about the middle, one in each hand, and, using them as weapons, stabbed each to death with the other. They kept attacking. Hitting him with such force that the ice chips flew, and he felt himself bruising inside his armor. But he kept catching the demons in his hands and two by two he stabbed them to death, using one against the other. Finally, those left alive retreated; they sped toward the castle to receive further orders from Boreas.

Whereupon Hercules proceeded with the rest of his plan. He fell to the ice and sprawled there, pretending to be too weak to arise. He lay still, waiting for an owl to attack. Sure enough, one of the great white birds, seeing him lie there, dived upon him, raking him with its meat-hook talons, stabbing with its beak. It chipped ice, but could not pierce it.

Hercules waited. Having wandered the beaches of his home-land all during his boyhood, he had become acquainted with seabirds, especially gulls, and one habit of theirs had kindled an idea. So he waited. The owl clutched him in its great talons, tried

When their pointed heads hit their targets—tree, wall, beast or armored man—they would pass right through and come out the other side.

to pull him into the air. Hercules felt himself being pulled, but he knew he was too heavy for one bird. He heard the owl scream, heard others scream in response. Felt the shock as they landed on him.

Then, four of them fastened their talons on him. Beating their great wings, they labored upward. What they meant to do, he knew, was to take him high then drop him, hoping to crack his icy carapace—just as gulls drop clams onto rocks to break their shells.

Up, up they flew, up above the top of the frozen rainbow. At that point, Hercules suddenly thrashed his arms and legs— kicked free, and dropped. Reaching as far as he could, he just managed to grasp the rainbow and clutch it fast. He balanced himself on the arch of colors and fought off the owls as they dived at him again.

He caught one by its beak, and with a whiplash movement broke its neck and flung it away. The others flew off, screaming. Hercules perched on the rainbow and fixed his eyes on the castle, waiting for Boreas to come out. He was one big bruise. Strangely enough, though, despite his casing of ice, his violent activity and the battle rage kept him warm.

He sat there, waiting. He knew that Boreas, when a wind, moved through the air as a vast disembodied force, too strong to be contained in any physique . . . but that when he came to earth resumed his Titan form. Nevertheless, Hercules gasped when he saw what emerged from the castle. For Boreas was perhaps the largest of all the Titans.

Wrapped in his black cape, he looked like a hundred-foot cedar tree moving over the ground. Hercules held very still. The owls were still screaming above him. And Boreas, hearing them scream, strode toward the foot of the rainbow. Closer and closer he came.

Hercules waited. And when Boreas neared the foot of the rainbow, Hercules moved. He arose and leaped. Encased in his massive ice armor, he fell a quarter of a mile toward the Titan, picked up speed as he went. And fell upon Boreas like a thunderbolt, knocking him into the permafrost, driving him under.

Blood spread beneath the ice—the curious pink blood, called *ichor*, which runs in the veins of gods and Titans. Hercules knew that, wounded as he was, Boreas would have trouble floundering up again. How much time, though, this would give him he did not know. He raced toward the castle, calling, "Iris! Iris!"

4

Daughter of the Rainbow

Iris was a very busy goddess. In addition to her after-storm duties she served as Hera's messenger. And was so sweet natured and obliging that all the gods had fallen into the habit of asking her to do favors for them. Her popularity also enabled her to act as peacemaker. And she flitted about Olympus, seeking to patch up the feuds that simmered like heat lightning about the crags of the sacred mountain.

For all her busyness, however, she took better care of her child than most goddesses. She managed to spend at least one day a week with Iole, and had arranged with the flower nymphs to care for the little girl the rest of the time. Iole was very fond of the sleek laughing creatures, and was happy dwelling among them. She missed her mother, nevertheless, and was overjoyed when the gorgeous young goddess came to visit her.

Her favorite times were when they perched on top of the rainbow together, telling each other things. The little girl was growing very clever, and her quality of listening had a way of drawing the stories out of Iris. She would chatter by the hour, telling tales of the gods and goddesses, their loves and their quar-

*Iole, daughter of the rainbow, grew
into a vivid girl—with curly red hair,
golden skin, and jade-green eyes.*

rels, and their adventures among mortals. And Iole would listen and listen, and never forgot anything she heard.

But her favorite story was the one Iris told about herself— about the time she was abducted by the North Wind, and her fear and loathing of the brutal Boreas, and how she had grieved during her captivity, and how she had been rescued by the young Hercules. That was a story Iole could not get enough of; she made her mother tell it again and again, and if she changed a word, made her correct herself and tell it exactly the way she had told it the first time.

Iole, daughter of the rainbow, grew into a vivid girl—with curly red hair, golden skin, and jade-green eyes. Her short tunics were dyed in the wildflower colors that her mother cast into the sky. And when she followed her mother, sliding joyously down the arch of colors, people watching below thought that a piece of the rainbow was breaking off.

Many a night the girl dreamed of the huge shy youth who had rescued her mother and melted the snow with his blushes when she tried to thank him with a kiss. And Iole resolved to make herself known to Hercules before she was twelve years old. As it happened, though, she was to meet him sooner than she expected.

Willem de Kooning *Woman, I.* (1950–52)

5

An Angry Goddess

era had summoned Hecate to Olympus. The two towering goddesses were conversing in the Garden of the Gods.

Hera said: "You know that Zeus has fettered us with a new law. No god, except for himself, of course, may kill more than five mortals a month. I, as Queen of the Gods, am allowed a larger quota—twelve. Now, that may sound sufficient but there's a tricky clause to the law. A demigod's life is valued at a much higher rate. And this is particularly irksome to me. I rarely concern myself with mortals; the chief targets of my wrath are demigods—as my husband well knows. For most demigods are his own children—by other females. That is why I hate them so. But I'm not allowed to kill any of these ill-begotten spawn without special permission from Zeus, who always denies me that permission."

"Nevertheless," said Hecate, "despite the law, demigods seem to be meeting with as many fatal accidents as they ever did."

"Yes," said Hera. "I've been able to contrive many such episodes. What I do is arrange for them to meet gigantic wild beasts and various monsters—encounters that they rarely survive. Which brings us to Hercules."

*"It's called the Hydra, and is the most dreadful of
the monstrous brood spawned by Typhon and Echidna."*

"Yes, Hercules," said Hecate. "We of the infernal regions
have been observing his career with much distaste."

"Distaste!" cried Hera. "Of all Zeus's slimy sons I hate him
the most. And am determined to kill him before the year is out."

"Anything we can do to help?" asked Hecate.

"Indeed, yes. That is why I asked you to come here. So far he's managed to vanquish everyone and everything I've sent against him—dragons and sea serpents and giants. What we need is something truly extraordinary in the way of monsters. And no one knows more about such matters than you do, oh Queen of Harpies."

"Offhand I can think of two who might do the trick," said Hecate. "The first that comes to mind is the Nemean Lion."

"Lion?" said Hera scornfully. "No good against Hercules. He kills them like rabbits."

"Not this one," said Hecate. "The Nemean Lion is very special. Big as an elephant. Its teeth are ivory daggers, its claws like razor-sharp baling hooks. And its hide cannot be pierced by sword, spear, or arrow."

"Sounds good," said Hera.

"The second is even more deadly. It's called the Hydra, and is the most dreadful of the monstrous brood spawned by Typhon and Echidna. It's a dragon basically, but much larger, and has a hundred heads. And each of these heads has a hundred teeth— hollow teeth from which it squirts poison, the most potent ever known. One drop of this venom will burn a hole through a bronze breastplate and scorch flesh from bone, roasting the warrior inside his armor in a matter of seconds. The Hydra is so strong that even without poison it would be completely invincible. With one flail of its spiked tail it can scythe down a grove of trees or shatter a stone wall."

"Sounds even better," said Hera, smiling. "Hercules will meet the Hydra first, and I'll save the lion for the next one on my hate list. I thank you, oh Hecate. Please do not hesitate to call upon me for any boon I may bestow."

"I thank you, oh Queen," said Hecate. "I'm sure the occasion will arise."

"Farewell. Convey my greetings to my brother Hades."

"Good hunting."

6

Iole's Plan

Iole, who had taught herself to speak with various animals, was frisking with a fawn that day, when a nymph came running up to tell her that Iris had come to the meadow. Iole dashed across the radiant grass, crying, "Mother! Mother!"

Passing through a fringe of trees she heard a sound of weeping, and was amazed to see that it was her mother—who never wept—sitting on a tree stump, sobbing.

"What's the matter, Mother? Why are you crying?"

"I'm grieved to the heart, Iole."

"Why . . . why?"

"Hercules is in dreadful danger," whispered Iris.

"But he's always in danger. That's what he does, fights dangerous things . . . and always wins."

"Not this time, I'm afraid."

"Why not? Why not?"

"Well, you know that I serve Hera, who is Hercules' worst enemy. And I have done this more willingly because I thought that one day I might learn something that would help him. And now I have. But what I've learned is so dreadful that I fear no one can help him. For the past few months, you see, Hera has been growing angrier and angrier. For not one of her attempts to kill Hercules has succeeded. Our brave young man has vanquished dragons, giants, and a murderous selection of wild beasts. And with every one of his triumphs Hera's temper has grown worse. Yesterday she sent me to the Underworld to fetch Hecate—and a dreadful trip it is, my child. Oh what agonies down below; how those poor shades are tormented in that ghastly realm. . . . Anyway, I did find Hecate, and gave her Hera's message. And when she came to Olympus this morning, I hid in the garden so that I might overhear their conversation. As I expected, Hera had sent for Hecate to seek her counsel. And that vicious Harpy was happy to oblige. She suggested two monsters that Hera might send against Hercules. And either one of them will finish him off.''

Iole had been stroking her mother's head all this time, and Iris had stopped weeping. Now the girl asked, "Can you describe those monsters to me, Mother?"

And Iris did. Iole listened very carefully. When Iris had finished, the girl asked, "Which one is he to fight first?"

"Oh, the Hydra—because it's the most deadly, and because Hera wants to kill our brave boy as soon as possible."

"Mother, I have an idea. Did you say that this lion has a hide that no weapon can pierce?"

"So Hecate says, my child."

"Listen then . . . ." And Iole began to explain her idea. But Iris clapped her hand over the girl's mouth.

"Hush," she whispered. "Not here! The vengeful Hera sends her tattle-birds everywhere. One of them may be hovering now, trying to hear what we say. And will fly back immediately to tell all she has heard. Come to the waterfall, Iole, where the sound of the falling water will cover your words."

The rainbow goddess and her daughter raced over the meadow to the waterfall. So light footed were they, the grass seemed scarcely to bend. Standing by the fall then, Iole explained her idea.

"Very clever indeed," said Iris. "But for it to work, Hera must change her schedule."

"That is up to you, Mother. You must find the wit to persuade her."

"Alas, my child, you get your beauty from me, but I had no wit to bequeath you. You get that from your father—who has little else to recommend him."

Iole furrowed her smooth brow, then smiled. "Mother, Mother, I think I know a way to persuade Hera. This is what you must say."

She glanced up to make sure no tattle-bird was hovering, then, taking no chances, she put her mouth to her mother's ear and whispered. . . .

"Yes, that might work," murmured Iris. "But let's go over it again a few times. Tell me exactly what to say."

"The vengeful Hera sends her tattle-birds everywhere."

"I will, Mother. And we'll rehearse it again and again until you get it right."

On Olympus the next day, Iris said to Hera, "I admire you for many things, my Queen, but most of all, perhaps, for your merciful nature."

Hera stared at her in astonishment. Being so powerful and dangerous a goddess, she was used to overblown compliments, even from those who loathed her. But the most ardent flatterer had never called her merciful.

"What do you mean?" she asked.

"I am delighted to know that you plan to spare Hercules much suffering."

"Do I? How?"

"Well," said Iris, "from my perch in the sky I have been able to observe both the Nemean Lion and the Hydra. They are both fearsome, of course, but of the two, the Hydra is worse. It's so poisonous that hounds sniffing at its footprints keel over and die. A single bite from any one of its ten thousand teeth kills instantly. Hercules won't last the wink of an eye against the Hydra, but against the Nemean Lion he would last longer. He could not prevail; he would be mauled, clawed, chewed. The lion, in fact, would play with him as a cat does a mouse, and he would die in agony. But now, thanks to your tender heart, he

Hera stared at her in astonishment.

will be spared that slow anguish. For he will not have to meet the lion, according to your plans. The Hydra will kill him first, and so quickly, so painlessly."

"Why is his fate of such interest to you?"

"Well, my Queen, you know that he saved me once, some years ago, while he was still a lad. When the North Wind abducted me, it was Hercules who came after us, who penetrated those icy wastes, combated legions of frost demons—had the incredible bravery to assault the North Wind himself, and was able to carry me back to safety. My heart swells with gratitude whenever I think of him."

"And mine with loathing," cried Hera. "Do you not know that he whom you praise is the creature I find most hateful in the entire world?"

"I know you do, Hera, I know you do. That is why I so much admire your compassion in allowing him you loathe so much to avoid great suffering by pitting him against the Hydra before he has to meet the terrible lion."

"I am afraid you have done your friend an ill service by speaking thus," said Hera, letting every word drop from her lips like distilled poison. "I have decided to reverse the order of events. He shall be thrown into the path of the lion first. Shall know those ripping talons, those enormous jaws full of dagger teeth. He shall be played with—slowly, excruciatingly—as a cat entertains itself with a mouse before killing it. Now, get out of my sight! I am very angry with you for still remembering with affection this mortal whom I hate and loathe and despise. Go—before you feel the full weight of my displeasure!"

Iris moved swiftly. Her draperies were a blur of color as she vanished from Hera's sight. But when she was alone, she laughed aloud. For she had accomplished her purpose. She had to follow this up, however, by making sure that Hercules would know what to do when he met the lion. She sped off then to find her daughter.

7

Blood Price

eus looked down upon earth and was displeased. He summoned Hermes and said: "I need your advice, Son. I have been observing my human herds and do not like what I see. The mortals I have most favored seem to be the most murderous. Kings, for example; they're always killing someone, including members of their own family."

"Yes, indeed," said Hermes. "To be a king's brother these days is almost fatal, particularly if you're the one next in line to the throne."

"It's getting monotonous, this mayhem," said Zeus. "How do you propose that I deal with it?"

"Blood price," said Hermes.

"What's that supposed to mean?"

"Honored Sire, I propose that you pass an edict forbidding murder within a family and impose a heavy fine upon anyone breaking that law."

"Fine? For a king?" exclaimed Zeus. "They have vast treasuries, and if they run short of funds, they simply rob their subjects through new taxes. No fine will discourage any king from braining his brother with a scepter."

*Hera knew that Hercules
spent part of each morning
practicing archery. . .*

"Make the penalty heavier then. Make your law say that anyone killing any member of his family within the second degree of cousinship must place himself in servitude to the head of that family for an entire year."

"But," said Zeus, "suppose a king, who is automatically head of his family, does the killing. Whom would he serve?"

"A neighboring king," said Hermes. "Which, by the nature of things, would put him at considerable risk."

Zeus guffawed. "There's a lot of meat in your idea, Son. I can see trouble administering such a law, but we'll work things out as we go along."

Hera was pleased by this new edict. Not that she had any distaste for killing, but she saw how the provisions of this law might help to solve her most urgent problem.

For she fully expected that one of the monsters proposed by Hecate would put an end to Hercules. His death, however, would cause a great sensation on earth, and in heaven. And she, Hera, known by all to have sworn vengeance against Hercules, would surely be suspected by Zeus, whose suspicions always hardened into certainty, and such certainties always turned into violence.

What she needed then was to contrive the young hero's death in a way that would absolve her of blame. And the new law suggested such a way.

She followed Hercules one day when he went out into the

woods. For she had studied his habits and knew that he spent part of each morning practicing archery and spear throwing. She guided him over the Theban frontier into Mycenae, a realm ruled by his cousin, King Eurystheus. She hovered invisibly as he shot arrows at a tree, bending the bow only halfway, for his full-armed pull would send an arrow through the tree. His hand flashed from quiver to bowstring, notching each shaft and letting it fly . . . each one planting itself exactly above the other so that a line of arrows, precisely one inch apart, climbed the tree.

While he was doing this, Hera had been misdirecting a party of young Mycenaeans out hunting. Princes they were, brothers and cousins of Eurystheus, the king. The merry youths were riding with a loose rein, laughing and chatting as their horses picked their way among the trees. Hera guided the horses toward Hercules, brought them within bowshot, and, as the archer shot his last arrow, Hera deflected it in midflight. It sailed past the tree and into the chest of a young prince, killing him instantly.

Hercules was horrified. He had no way of knowing that Hera had deflected his arrow; the idea never occurred to him. Innocently, he thought that he had missed his aim, that his own poorly shot arrow had killed the prince. Roaring with grief, he burst out of the brush and rushed to where the man lay, tore open his tunic, and examined the wound. But the man was dead.

The others sat their horses in utter shock, staring at the gigantic young stranger, who was shouting and sobbing, accusing himself of criminal carelessness, and offering to pay the blood price.

Hera, still hovering invisibly, uttered a snarling laugh. "Now," she said to herself, "I'll visit King Eurystheus in a dream and instruct him to extort the blood price from Hercules—to become, in fact, his taskmaster for the space of a year. But it won't take a year, not even a month. For the first task I'll make him give the lout will be to slay the Nemean Lion. And we know who'll slay whom. Yes, Hercules will die now, and his death will be entirely legal. No one will be able to blame me."

8

New Girl at the Palace

ris and Iole perched on the rainbow, gazing down at a drenched meadow sparkling in the slanting rays of the sun. The daughter looked excited; her mother was trying to look cheerful.

"It won't do," said Iris. "You're simply too vivid to pass unnoticed in the Mycenaean court. We'll have to tone you down, my girl."

"How?"

"Can't do much about your eyes or your skin. But we'll have to darken your hair."

"Whatever you say, Mother."

"You'll be able to wash the dye out when you come home . . ."

"Don't worry about it. I'm not."

"Let's slide down and get you attended to by the nymphs."

They slid down the arch of colors, but neither of them sang joyously this time. When they reached the meadow and were greeted by the nymphs, Iris spoke privately to Numa, who listened earnestly and then took Iole's arm and led her to the far end of the glade where the dyeing vats stood.

The nymph dropped a handful of roots into clear boiling water. The water thickened, foamed, went black. Numa took a pair of silver shears and began to cut Iole's hair. It was a glorious red-gold mane, hanging down to her waist. Numa cut it so that it barely reached the girl's shoulders, then cut bangs. Finally, when the dye had cooled, she blackened Iole's hair.

Iole dashed to a stream, knelt, and looked at herself. She squealed in excitement and raced across the meadow to Iris. "Mother, Mother, look!"

Iris took her daughter by the shoulders and gazed down at her, winking back a tear.

"How do I look, Mother?"

"Like a cat, my dear. With those black bangs and jade-green eyes you look exactly like an Egyptian temple cat."

"But quite unnoticeable, don't you think? I'll be able to slink around the Mycenaean court like a shadow and help Hercules all I please without anyone knowing. Don't you think so, Mother? Who pays much attention to a black cat, after all?"

"But you will be very careful, won't you, my child? Eurystheus is an exceedingly cruel king. And while he's very stupid himself, he's surrounded by crafty councillors. So take no unnecessary chances."

"I won't, Mother. I'll go there, find Hercules and do what I have to do. Then I'll come right back. I swear."

"Farewell then, dear girl . . . brave darling girl . . . " Iris ran off then so that Iole would not see her weep.

The girl then shed her rainbow draperies, and donned a plain brown tunic. She bade farewell to the nymphs and set off for the court of Eurystheus.

Iole had no experience of the mortal world, no idea of how anything worked . . . and when she wanted something, she went after it with utter simplicity.

On reaching Mycenae, she went directly to the royal palace, melted into the shadows, and observed things for a while. It was

*It was a very broad, long stairway, and
extremely dirty. . . . Because the king often rode
his horse up the stairs to his bedchamber.*

midmorning; the king had not yet awakened, and seven maids
with seven mops were swabbing a flight of marble stairs. Every
so often, one of them would take the bucket of dirty water away
and return with clean water. This meant carrying the heavy
wooden bucket out to a well in the courtyard and drawing water.
While she was gone, the other maids leaned on their mops and
chatted, and slowly, with many groans and sighs, began to mop
again when she came back. For these servants were not young,
and it was a very broad, long stairway, and extremely dirty.
Because the king often rode his horse up the stairs to his
bedchamber.

The next time the water needed changing, Iole flashed out
of the shadows, swung the bucket up, and ran out. She took her
time about drawing water from the well, for the sun was shining
brightly and the birds were singing . . . and she knew that the
moppers would welcome a rest. Then she trotted back, swinging

the bucket lightly, took a mop from the eldest servant and joined the others. Since she was very strong and quick and did as much work by herself as the other six together, she was made welcome and no one questioned her presence. They all thought she was simply another servant girl taken on by the majordomo.

By the time the king descended, the enormous stairway was spotless. The servants stood with their face to the wall as the king passed. They had been trained to do that, because the king did not like to look at servants. This suited Iole, for she wished to attract as little attention as possible. But she did sneak a glance over her shoulder as he went by, and gasped with surprise. Eurystheus was not what she thought a king should look like. He

A group of courtiers had gathered in the reception hall and followed the king into the great dining hall where breakfast was served.

was enormously fat, with a triple paunch and a multitude of chins. His face was red and bloated; his nose was a snout; he wheezed and grunted as he waddled down the stairs.

By this time a group of courtiers had gathered in the reception hall and followed the king into the great dining hall where breakfast was served. Iole slipped among the horde of servants who were busy bringing in the breakfast, bearing great platters of food from the kitchen to the dining hall. And again she proved herself so swift and graceful, and bore the heavy platters with such ease, that she was welcomed among the servants and no one challenged her right to be there.

After a few days Iole felt that she was fully accepted; it was as if she had worked in the palace all her life. And she began to plan her next move.

Now, the juiciest topic of gossip in the court was Hercules, who had come and gone a week before. How the king had feared his coming, and stationed soldiers beyond the castle walls so that he might be warned when Hercules approached. How a soldier had rushed into the throne room, crying, "I have seen him, oh King! He approaches the wall. And he's gigantic!" And how, when the king heard this, his red face had turned a ghastly purplish white, and he quivered like a great pudding. "Don't let him enter!" he bellowed. "Don't let him pass through the gate! Copreus! Copreus! Where the hell is Copreus? Oh, there you are. Copreus, you go and relay my wishes to Hercules. Tell him he must slay the Nemean Lion and bring me its hide. But meet him outside the walls. Run! Run!"

Copreus rushed way. Awaiting his return, the king had behaved like a madman, gnawing his knuckles, roaring at people, hurling his scepter at them, threatening this one and that one with execution before the day was out. He quieted down only when Copreus returned and described his meeting with Hercules.

"He *is* huge, Your Majesty," Copreus had said. "About nine feet tall and with shoulders like a span of oxen. But very

gentle. He greeted me courteously, and listened quietly as I told him what you wanted him to do. And received the news calmly. 'Tell the king I thank him for his confidence in me,' he said. 'And when I return with the lion's hide, I hope to meet him personally.' And he strode off."

"That big, eh?" said the king. "You don't think he has a chance against the lion, do you?"

"Oh, my lord," said Copreus. "No chance at all. A hunting party went out against that lion in Nemea, I'm told. Tested men, warriors all, the strongest archers and spearmen in the land. The lion stood under a shower of spears and arrows, and they were like a fall of dry leaves. The beast wasn't even scratched. Then he charged and killed the huntsmen, every one. Their bones lie bleaching in the Valley of Nemea."

"Very well," said the king. "But set the sentries. Station lookouts on the road to Nemea. When Hercules is killed I want the tidings of his death relayed to me without an instant's delay."

And," said the old woman who was pretending to dust a vase as she whispered to Iole, "he's been waiting several days, and going crazier each day. . . . Oh, my goodness, listen to that!"

For the king was shouting in the throne room: They could hear his scepter clattering on the marble floor. Copreus rushed out, pale and trembling. He looked about frantically, then beckoned to Iole. "You there—girl! Come here!"

"Me, sir?"

"Yes, you! Quickly, I say!"

Iole went to him. "You have long legs," said Copreus. "You look like you can run fast. Can you?"

"Yes, sir."

"I can't send a horseman; the way lies through thick brush. Do you know the hill that lies a mile to the east, beyond the oak called the Gallows Tree?"

"Yes."

"Halfway up that hill you'll find a cave. Within that cave you'll see little people making clothes. Don't ask any questions now—run, run!"

"Just one question, sir. What shall I do when I get there?"

"Oh, yes. Of course. You are to tell the head tailor to come here as quickly as he can. Perhaps you'd better carry him because he has very short legs. Bring him back here. For the king wants new ceremonial robes by tomorrow afternoon. And if he doesn't get them my head will fall on the block. I've never seen him in such a state. Anxiety about Hercules, of course, but whatever it is, it means the axe for me if he doesn't get his damned robes by tomorrow. Run, girl, run!"

"I'm off, sir."

Iole dashed away.

9

The Little Tailors

ole stood at the mouth of the cave, trying to see inside. The light was tricky. Rush torches stood in niches in the wall and cast flickering shadows. The sounds were confusing, too. A busy, scolding hub-bub: She couldn't distinguish any words, nor could she see who was uttering the sounds.

She moved farther into the cave. There was a rush, a rustling—then a deep pulsing silence. Iole stared in amazement. The place seemed to be inhabited by headless statues. She went among them. They weren't statues; they were stuffed cloth figures, male and female. They were draped with scraps of tunics, gowns, hunting costumes, court robes. In a space all its own stood an enormously fat figure, clad in a half-finished cloak of royal purple.

"The king!" whispered Iole to herself, and realized what she was seeing. These figures were tailors' dummies, representing all the nobles of the Mycenaean court. The fat one was the king.

She heard another rushing sound, the patter of footsteps, a thin babble of voices. Something clutched her tunic. She looked down. She was surrounded by a swarm of tiny people. Men and women alike wore leather aprons. The men were bearded, the women wore their hair very long. The tallest of them didn't quite reach to her waist.

This one was jumping up and down in a fury, shouting at Iole. "Who are you? Why have you come here?"

He turned to the others. "To work! To work!"

Iole paid no attention to the raging little fellow but gazed in wonder as the others began to work. It was a most curious sight. The men plucked long hairs out of their beard and wound them on a kind of bobbin. The women pulled hairs out of their head and did the same thing. And Iole realized that their hair was thread. They cut cloth with their teeth, which were seemingly as sharp as scissor blades. Click, click, click, they bit the cloth, shearing it cleanly to the shapes they wanted as they clambered up onto the dummies. Perching there, they draped cloth over the figures, cut with their teeth, and sewed with both hands and feet. For they were barefooted and clutched long needles with their toes as well as with their hands . . .

The little head tailor was still hopping and shouting, and pushing now at Iole's legs, trying to shove her out of the cave. "Get out, get out, get out! You see how busy we are. And we don't welcome strangers."

Iole made her voice as deep as she could. "I come by order of the king," she said. "Copreus sent me. You are to come to the palace immediately and make ceremonial robes for the king. He wants them by tomorrow afternoon."

"Tomorrow afternoon? Impossible! Besides, we just made him ceremonial robes—just last week."

"They don't fit," said Iole. "It seems he's gained twenty pounds this week. I have no time to argue with you. Come on."

"Impossible I tell you."

"Tell it to Copreus," she said.

She scooped him up, tucked him under her arm, and ran out of the cave.

"Stop!" he cried. "Stop!" He kicked and waved his arms.

"Hush—or I'll smack you!"

"Don't you dare, you wicked bullying girl. I can't stand pain."

"Well, you'll have to stand it if you don't hush. But I'm afraid you won't be able to sit for a while."

He must have believed she meant what she said because he stopped kicking and uttered no sound. She giggled and ran faster. She was feeling very happy, very lucky. For she suddenly saw how these magical little tailor folk might fit right into her plans for helping Hercules—if he only helped himself first by vanquishing the terrible lion.

10

The Lion's Hide

he little tailors had indeed finished the king's garments by the next afternoon, and Copreus felt his head resting more securely on his shoulders. But not for long.

The next day a horseman came thundering into the courtyard. He reined up when he saw Copreus, and cried, "He's done it, sir!"

"Who's done what?"

"Hercules! He's killed the Nemean Lion."

"Are you sure?"

"Shepherds brought us word. They were pasturing their flocks on the Nemean hills and saw six vultures feasting on a carcass. It had no head or hide, but it was so enormous that it had to be that lion. It's good news, isn't it, sir? Just what the king wanted, isn't it?"

"Yes, of course," said Copreus. "And I'm about to do you a great favor, young man, one that will advance your career considerably. I'm going to let *you* bear this good news to the king. He'll probably promote you on the spot, and give you a rich bonus."

But the guardsman didn't hear the last sentence. He had

*The guardsman wheeled his horse
and galloped out of the courtyard.*

wheeled his horse and galloped out of the courtyard. This did not surprise Copreus. He knew that everyone feared the king. He went slowly toward the throne room, trying to prepare himself for the worst. For he fully expected to receive a skull-shattering blow from the king's scepter before he finished his tale.

Eurystheus was staring at him as he approached the throne, bowing deeply. He couldn't read the expression on the king's fat face. "Sire," he cried. "The people of Nemea are hailing you as their savior."

"Are they?" asked Eurystheus. "Why?"

"Because of the young hero you sent them. He has slain the Nemean Lion that has been terrorizing the countryside."

"I warned Hera," muttered the king. "I advised her to let him fight the Hydra first because it is more deadly by far."

"What's the Hydra, Sire?"

"A monster that will be Hercules' second task, and should have been his first. Listen carefully now because you are to meet this accursed hero outside the gates and give him his assignment."

"But, Your Majesty, he'll want to meet you personally. He told me before he left that he wished to receive your thanks when he returned with the lion's hide."

"I won't see him! I won't," bellowed the king. "Make some excuse. Tell him anything, I don't care. Meet him outside the walls and dispatch him immediately upon his next task. Be clever now. Try to use your head while it's still on your shoulders. Convey to him my gratitude for his great deed, and assure him that I'll thank him in person when he comes back after killing the Hydra. Which he won't do, of course, if I can believe Hera."

"What is this Hydra exactly? I'll have to describe it to Hercules."

"I'll tell you what Hera told me."

And Eurystheus described the Hydra to Copreus, who felt his bones turning to jelly as he listened. He didn't linger in the throne room. He bowed his way

Copreus went slowly toward the throne room, trying to prepare himself for the worst.

out. By the time he reached his own chambers he was reeling with despair.

"Oh my," he moaned. "When I try to tell Hercules about this horrible beast, he'll take me between those big hands of his and twist my neck like a chicken. On the other hand, if I don't tell him, I won't have any head for him to twist off, because the king will cut it off. Woe is me . . . Woe . . . Woe . . . "

"Don't be sad, sir," said a voice.

He whirled around. It was Iole.

"How did you get here?" he cried.

"I followed you from the throne room. I wanted to tell you not to be sad because I'll go tell Hercules about the Hydra."

"You? What do you know about that monster?"

"I was in the throne room, hiding behind the throne. I heard what the king said to you."

"What do you mean sneaking around, eavesdropping, you little fool? Do you know what will happen if the king catches you?"

"Oh, he's too full of himself to notice anyone else. Besides, that old throne room is full of shadows. And it's hard to see me when I'm hiding."

"But Hercules is a very dangerous fellow. He's liable to get furious when he hears what his next task is to be."

"He won't hurt me. He likes children."

"How can you possibly know that?"

"I know . . . "

When Hercules came to Mycenae bearing a huge bundle that was the hide of the Nemean Lion, he found the gates locked against him. He thought about ripping them off their hinges, but decided not to. Instead, he camped outside the city. He thrust his spear into the ground, draped the lion hide over it, making a big tent, and went to sleep.

When he awoke the next morning, he found a child waiting outside his tent—a curious cat-faced girl who stared at him with enormous green eyes. He stared back. He saw that she was trying to look very serious but couldn't quite do it because her face was brimming with glee.

"Good morning, Missy," he said.

"My name is Iole. And you are Hercules, prince of Thebes, champion of mortal against monster, and vanquisher of the Nemean Lion whose hide now serves as your tent."

Hercules shook his head in wonder. "How old are you?"

"I'm not sure," said Iole. "We don't do that kind of counting where I come from. I'm supposed to be quite young though. Not old enough to be married yet, if that's what you mean."

"I don't mean that at all," said Hercules.

"But I'm ready to be betrothed."

"Are you? To whom?"

"To you, of course," said Iole.

"To me?"

"What you must do is ask me to marry you. And I'd say yes. And you'd tell me you know I'm too young but you'd gladly wait till I'm old enough. That's how you do it."

"You're an amazing child. Very pretty, and almost too clever. But I'm in no position to ask anyone to wait for me. In this line of work, I don't figure to last too long."

"Oh, I'll help you with your work."

Hercules stared back.

"How?"

"That's what I've come to do now."

"What do you mean?"

"First of all, I'm the one who comes from Eurystheus to tell you what your next task will be."

"My dear girl, you have a very nimble imagination. The one who assigns me my tasks is the king's doer of dirty jobs, one named Copreus."

"I know, I know, but not this time. For what you must do next is so dreadful that Copreus was afraid you'd kill him on the spot when he told you about it. So he sent me instead."

"Sent you? What kind of man is he?"

"Not bad in some ways. A coward, of course. But the king is worse. Don't you want me to tell you about your next task?"

"I take it you're not afraid of me?"

"Not a bit. Should I be?"

"No. Go ahead with your story. I'm prepared for the worst."

"Oh, it's as bad as can be all right," said Iole cheerfully. "You are to go to Argos, to a river named Lerna, where dwells the Hydra."

"And what may that be?"

"The last word in fearsomeness. A kind of dragon basically. Seems to have a hundred heads though, every one of them filled with teeth. And one flail of its spiked tail can mow down a phalanx of armored men. It eats a pastureful of cattle in one meal, plus any herdsmen who happen to be around. It spits out sheep because it doesn't like the taste of wool, but leaves them dead, nevertheless. In fact, the people of Argos are in a very bad way because of this monster and have sent their bravest warriors against it. And not one of them came back."

"This thing dwells in the river Lerna, you say?"

"It hunts during the day and sleeps in the river at night. And comes out again in the morning."

"Very well. Thank you. I'm off."

"So soon?" asked Iole.

"It's my task, you say. The sooner you get to these things, the sooner they're over."

"No sir," cried Iole. "You can't go yet."

"What do you mean? Why not?"

"There's something that must be done first."

"What?"

"One item I forgot to mention about the Hydra is that each of its hundred heads has a hundred teeth—hollow teeth. And they're hollow because he squirts poison through them, a venom that kills instantly. One scratch from any one of those teeth and you'll be dead before you hit the ground."

"What do you suggest, that I duck this fight? I don't do that."

"Oh, no," said Iole. "I know you don't. That tent you're living in—it *is* the hide of the Nemean Lion, isn't it?"

"Yes, my dear. It is."

"And it's unpierceable by any weapon, is it not?"

"True. Even my weapons could not pierce it—not arrow, nor spear, nor sword."

"Well, I want to know all about how you managed to kill it, of course. But you'll have time to tell me as we go."

"As we go? What do you mean?"

"Never mind that for now. What I want to suggest is that you make that hide into a suit of armor, and wear it when you fight the Hydra. That way his poison teeth won't be able to pierce you."

"But I never fight in armor. It's too hot. And it doesn't let me move freely."

"You've never fought a Hydra before either. Don't you see, you *must* wear the armor. Don't you want to kill that monster? Or do you want him to kill you? Do you want all the cattle of Argos to keep on being eaten as all the people starve? You must make a jacket and trousers of the hide, and a pair of boots. Gauntlets, too. Every inch of your skin must be covered. And you can wear its skull as a helmet and look out its eyeholes."

"That will take a lot of tailoring, little girl."

"And I know where there's a lot of tailors. A whole cave full. Magical ones, who can make your armor in one day. Roll up that hide and follow me. You'll have your lion-skin armor by tomorrow."

He looked down at her without moving.

"Don't think I'm bossy," she cried. "Please don't. I came to Mycenae from a very far place just to save you. And worked as a servant in the palace, mopping a filthy staircase because that fat lazy slob of a king rides his horse up and down it. Please, Hercules, come with me and get your armor made. You've almost promised to marry me someday, and you can't if you're not alive. I may be about to cry."

"No, no, don't do that!" roared Hercules. "Don't cry."

He snatched the lion hide off the spear that was its tent pole, rolled it up with the skull inside, hoisted it to his shoulder, scooped Iole up, and set her on his other shoulder. "We'll make better time this way," he said. "Just show me how to go."

Hercules was too tall to fit into the cave. So the tailors moved outside. They used their entire work force, and Hercules served as his own dummy. He stood stock-still as the thread-haired, scissor-toothed little folk climbed all over him, measuring, draping. They couldn't do any sewing because no needle would pierce the lion hide. They used an extraordinarily powerful glue, brewed by themselves for tough leather garments.

All this time, Iole prowled about the glade, watching closely to make sure that everything was done the way she wanted— that the suit of armor covered Hercules from head to toe, which included fitting the lion-skull helmet and making lion-hide boots. But the head tailor, who had never forgiven Iole for carrying him off the first time, objected.

"No helmet, no boots," he hissed. "We're not hatters or cobblers, you know."

Iole studied the sullen little fellow for a moment and wasted no time arguing. She snatched him up and, holding him upside down by the ankles—the way a butcher holds a goose—walked to where Hercules was standing and asked, "Are you hungry, sir?"

"I could eat something," said Hercules . . . "How about you?"

"Your breakfast will be served shortly, sir."

She bore the head tailor into the cave, took him to the cave end where the tiny folk did their cooking, swung him onto a stone slab, and slowly began to unhook his tunic.

"Help! Help!" he shrieked, but there was no one to hear but Iole. She held him down with the palm of her hand and fixed her green eyes upon him.

"What are you doing?" he screamed.

Iole studied the sullen little fellow for a moment and wasted no time arguing.

"Trying to decide how to do you. He's a meat eater, you know. Prefers it roasted, usually, but you look pretty tough and stringy. Probably need boiling. Where do you keep the salt and pepper?"

"Please, please, don't cook me. I don't want to be eaten."

"Don't want to feed a guest? That's not very polite."

"Oh, mercy. . . . Feed him something else. Please!"

"Will you do everything I say?"

"Yes, yes, everything!"

"Helmet and boots?"

"Exactly as you want them, dear girl."

"All right. But don't make any more mistakes. This is your last chance."

She lifted her hand then. He squirmed away and scrambled off the slab—rushed out, shouting, "Boots and helmet! Get to work! Quickly, quickly!"

Iole came out of the cave, smiling.

Finally, the work was done. Hercules stood in the glade like a gigantic lion rearing up on its hind legs. Iole stalked about him, inspecting the armor.

"Hurry up," he said, his voice muffled by the helmet. "I'm sweltering in here."

"Looks good," called Iole. "Come on out."

He doffed the armor, bundled it up, thanked the tailor folk courteously for their labors, and turned to Iole.

"And I thank you, little girl," he said. "And when I come back from Argos—if I do—I shall tell you all about my fight with the Hydra, and about my fight with the lion before that."

"Oh, you'll have time to tell me the lion story on our way to Argos," said Iole. "I'm going with you, you know."

"No you're not."

"I am. I want to."

"Do you think I'd let you go anywhere near that dreadful monster?"

She stamped her foot. "I want to go! I want to go!"

He heard the tears behind her voice. He lifted her then and set her on the branch of a tree so that they could be face to face. Holding her by the shoulders, he said:

"Listen to me, Iole. This Hydra sounds more dangerous than any creature I've ever faced. Which means that I'll have to give every bit of my attention to the fight. And I won't be able to do that if you're there, because I'd be worrying about you. Your presence would put me in more peril than if I were to face the beast without any armor at all. Is that what you want?"

She winked back her tears. "No-o-o. . . . "

"Very well, then. Wait for me in Mycenae. And if I live, I'll come back to see you. I promise."

He kissed her gently on the forehead and loped off. She looked after him, trying not to weep because the little folk were still there, looking up at her.

"This is ridiculous," she said to herself. "I can't bear it. I won't try to. I'll follow him there. He won't even know it."

She climbed down the tree and raced after Hercules, keeping him in sight but taking care not to be seen herself.

11

The Hydra

rees run down to the bank of the river Lerna. Water nibbles their roots and the trees lean over to watch their reflection in the shining river. At one point, though, the tree line stops short, and grass grows between river and wood.

It was in this meadow that Hercules stood. He wanted a clear view of the river. For it was from there that the Hydra would come. It was early upon a summer morning but the sun was already a brass ball, flaming hot. The young man felt himself slowly broiling inside the thick lion hide.

"It better come out soon," he thought. "Or it won't find anyone to fight—just a breakfast, all cooked and ready to eat."

Now the last monster Hercules had fought, the Nemean Lion, had announced itself by roaring so loudly that the boulders shook. Hercules didn't know that evil has more variety than goodness, and that monsters differ. So, waiting for some kind of horrid sound, he was almost caught off his guard. For the Hydra came with a faint scraping and was slithering swiftly across the grass before he saw it.

It was a crocodile, but the size of ten crocodiles. "This can't be it," thought Hercules. "It has only one head. But how many monsters that size can dwell in the river?"

Happy that he had only one head to cope with, big as that one was, he cast aside bow and spear and held only his sword. The Hydra scuttled toward him with astounding speed. Weighed down as he was by the heavy pelt, Hercules leaped straight up, turning in the air, and landed at the Hydra's shoulder. He raised his sword in a two-handed grip, and struck down in a tremendous shearing blow that cut through hard leather scales, through bone and muscle and flesh, slicing the head off so swiftly that it jumped off the neck. Blood spouted, a black vile broth that scorched the grass where it fell.

And Hercules was shocked to see the severed head turn and slide back toward him, rising from the ground and snapping its jaws in the air. Hercules struck it down with his clenched fist,

*It was a crocodile,
        but the size of ten crocodiles.*

whirled to face the Hydra again, and was horrified by what he saw. The stories were true; he had congratulated himself too soon. For the stump of neck had split into two; from each sprouted a new head.

Two heads now. Hercules charged, struck, cut off the new heads. They fell to the grass, but stayed alive, snapping about his legs like vicious hounds. They could not pierce his lion-skin trousers, but they clamped their jaws on his legs and tried to drag him down. And now, where there had been two heads, there were four.

Four heads struck at him with sickening force. Four sets of enormous jaws fastened on his arms. The awful teeth could not pierce the pelt, but Hercules felt them slowly crushing his bones. He tried to raise his sword, but could not; his arms were held by the jaws. He tore himself away, staggering, as the cut-off heads pulled at his legs. He fell to his knees, kicked free, and his sword became a glittering blur as he whirled it, cutting the heads off, one after the other.

But where the four heads had been, there were now eight. They came at him from all sides. Again they closed upon his arms and shoulders. Jaws clamped his midriff. He felt his ribs caving in. Jaws locked his head. They did not pierce the lion skull, but they were crushing it, and crushing his own head inside.

Worst of all, though, he saw that one of the new heads was spitting fire. The lion skin turned the flame, but he felt himself growing unbearably hot inside his armor. He could hardly breathe. With a desperate effort, he whirled and kicked and struck, hacked and stabbed. The cut-off heads ravened about him, clamping on his legs, pulling him down. The Hydra struck with a single head. In an instinctive counterstroke, which he instantly wished to recall, Hercules swung his sword again, shearing off that head. Two heads sprouted in its place. Now, he knew, there were too many heads for him to combat; he could fight no longer.

With the last flaring of strength, he caught up a fallen bough from the grass, held it in front of the fire-spitting head. The dead wood kindled immediately. Hercules sprang up with his torch in one hand, his sword in the other. He sliced off a head and seared the neck-stump with his torch. A hideous stench of roasting flesh fouled the air, but no head sprouted from the seared stump. Now, he knew, if he could only keep striking with sword and torch, cutting off heads and searing stumps, he might have a chance. But all the severed heads were upon him, a multitude of them now, fastening their jaws upon his legs, dragging him down.

Hercules knew there were too many heads for him to combat; he could fight no longer.

Iole, watching from behind a tree, saw him fall. She flashed out, raced across the grass, scooped up the fallen torch. Using it as a club she beat off the severed heads that were fastened to Hercules' legs. She thrust the sword at him, crying: "Cut off the heads and I'll burn the stumps! Get up! Get up!"

He looked up at her. Dazed as he was, he realized that she was clad only in her short tunic. One scratch of a poisoned tooth would kill her on the spot. Her peril filled him with fresh energy. He leaped up, snatched the torch from her; with his other hand seized her about the waist and hurled her across the meadow— into the river. He held torch in one hand, sword in the other, and crouched as the Hydra came at him.

He was afire now. His veins ran with starry wrath. He whirled and leaped, spun, dodged, weaved—striking as he moved, ducking the jaws, darting in, striking again. Each blow of his sword cut off a head. Then, striking with his torch, he immediately seared the stump so that no new head could sprout.

A dizzying mist arose from the spilled blood. Hercules peered through and saw that the Hydra had two heads left. He charged the monster and struck again, and again. He thrust twice with his torch, searing the last two stumps. Now the Hydra was blind. Its armored body twitched violently; its neck stumps were great charred worms, still wriggling. But it was dying. The body stopped twitching, the necks stopped wriggling. The spiked tail ceased its flailing. And as the huge body died, its fallen heads died also.

All this time, Hera had been hovering overhead, watching the battle, rejoicing when Hercules fell, filling with thwarted fury when she saw him arise and kill the Hydra.

"All the fault of that meddlesome brat," she hissed to herself. "I'll teach her a lesson."

Hera descended, reached into the river, pulled out a great tangle of drowned tree roots. She breathed life into them and they became a huge crab, big as a chariot wheel. She dropped the crab into the water. It sank swiftly, and began to crawl over

Hercules sprang up with his torch in one hand, his sword in the other.

the river bottom, hunting its food. Spotting something above, it rose to the surface and fastened its claws on Iole's leg. She screamed.

Hercules heard the scream. He charged toward the river, kicking through the litter of dead, grinning heads. He reached the river, dived in, seized the crab, and broke off the claw that held Iole. As she climbed upon the bank, Hercules arose, holding the crab. He dropped it to the grass and stamped on it, crushing it under his foot.

Iole threw herself into his arms. He hugged her to him, then shoved her away, crying, "Crazy girl! Sweet brave crazy wicked child! I don't know whether to kiss you or spank you."

"Better let me decide," she purred.

Catlike, she sprang into his lap and wrapped her arms about his neck. "You have many tasks before you," she murmured. "Please try to last a few more years—at least until I'm old enough to marry you."

"How many years will that be?" he asked.

"Four, perhaps. Three, if I hurry. . . . Let's go swimming before the sun sets. We're very smoky and bloody."

Hera could bear to hear no more. She flew off in a fury, vowing to avenge herself upon both of them, no matter how long it took. And, it is said, she put together the crushed crab, named it Cancer, and stuck it in the sky as a sign of her vengeance.

But something better happened in another part of the sky. Pieces of Iris's frozen rainbow still burn above the North Wind's castle, and are called the Northern Lights. Boreas, when he remembers what happened long ago, flies into a rage again and tries to blow them out . . . but never can.

Acknowledgments

Letter Cap Illustrations by Hrana L. Janto

Cover, THE SECOND LABOUR OF HERCULES: THE LERNAEAN HYDRA *(1983) by Earl Staley, acrylic on canvas (64 × 48")*
  Courtesy of William and Virginia Camfield, Houston

Opposite page 1, DEATH ON A PALE HORSE *by William Blake (1757–1827), pen and watercolor over pencil (39.5 × 31.1 cm.)*
  Courtesy of the Fitzwilliam Museum, Cambridge, England

Page 3, TROPICAL STORM WITH A TIGER *by Henri Rousseau (1844–1910), oil on canvas (129.8 × 161.9 cm.)*
  Courtesy of the National Gallery, London
    Photo: Bridgeman/Art Resource, NY

Page 6, DISCUS THROWER *(ca. 580 B.C.), Greek amphora*
  Courtesy of the National Museum, Naples
    Photo: Scala/Art Resource, NY

Page 8, POLAR BEAR *(1988) by Paul Schulze, formed by hand from a single gather of glass (27 1/2 × 5")*
  Courtesy of Steuben Glass, NY

Page 11, THE GARDEN *by Pierre Bonnard (1867–1947), oil on canvas*
  Courtesy of the Musée du Petit-Palais, Paris
    Photo: Giraudon/Art Resource, NY

Page 12, THE GREAT RED DRAGON AND THE WOMAN CLOTHED WITH THE SUN *(ca. 1805–10) by William Blake, watercolor (15 3/4 × 12 3/4")*
  Courtesy of the National Gallery, Washington, DC
    Photo: Scala/Art Resource, NY

Page 14, NAKED WATER *by Yves Tanguy (1900–1955), oil on canvas*
  Courtesy of the Joseph H. Hirshhorn Museum, Washington, DC
    Photo: Joseph Martin/Art Resource, NY

Page 16, BLUE HORSE WITH RAINBOW *(1913) by Franz Marc, watercolor, gouache, and pencil on paper (6 3/8 × 10 1/8")*
  Courtesy of the Museum of Modern Art, NY; John S. Newberry Collection

Page 20, *Untitled gouache and collage by Max Ernst (1891–1976)*
    Photo: Giraudon/Art Resource, NY

Page 22, CASTLE OF DREAMS *(1986) by David Dowler, molded sculpture of solid crystal, textured and polished (6 1/8 × 10 5/8")*
Courtesy of Steuben Glass, NY

Page 24, THE ANGEL OF LIFE *by Giovanni Segantini (1858–1899), oil on canvas*
Courtesy of Arte Moderna, Milan
Photo: Scala/Art Resource, NY

Page 26, AT VESPERS, *detail by Frederick Sandys (1829–1904), oil on panel (23 1/2 × 19 1/2")*
Courtesy of the FORBES Magazine Collection, NY
Photo: Larry Stein

Page 28, WOMAN, I. *(1950–52) by Willem de Kooning, oil on canvas (72 3/7 × 58")*
Courtesy of the Museum of Modern Art, NY; Purchase

Page 30, HERCULES AND THE HYDRA *by Gustave Moreau (1826–1898), oil on canvas (175.3 × 154 cm.)*
Courtesy of the Art Institute of Chicago; Gift of Mrs. Eugene A. Davidson, 1964.231. © 1988 the Art Institute of Chicago

Page 32, WOMAN WEEPING *by Pablo Picasso (1881–1973), oil on canvas*
Courtesy of the Sir Roland Penrose Collection, London
Photo: Bridgeman/Art Resource, NY

Page 35, PARROTS, *detail of a brocaded cloth, silk and metal thread, Italian (13th century)*
Courtesy of the Metropolitan Museum of Art; Fletcher Fund, 1946 (46.156.30)
Photo: Linton Gardiner

Page 36, EYE OF THE DIVA, *detail (1983) by Emilio Cruz, oil on canvas (7 × 7")*
Courtesy of the artist

Page 38, CAIN KILLING ABEL *by Guido Reni (1575–1642), oil on canvas*
Courtesy of Kunsthistorisches, Vienna
Photo: Kaveler/Art Resource, NY

Page 40, SORRA SHOOTING AT A MARK *(1561), Italian medal (diameter 2")*
Courtesy of the Metropolitan Museum of Art; Robert F. Lehman Collection, 1975 (1975.1.1261)

Page 42, PORTRAIT OF BEATRICE CENCI *by Guido Reni, oil on canvas*
Courtesy of the National Gallery, Rome
Photo: Alinari/Art Resource, NY

Page 45, ARCHITECTURAL STUDY FOR THE ADORATION OF THE MAGI *by Leonardo da Vinci (1452–1519), pen, ink, and gouache on paper*
Courtesy of Gabinetto Disegni, Florence
Photo: Scala/Art Resource

Page 46, BANQUET SCENE, *detail from* CONVITO DI ASSUERO *by Jacopo del Sellajo (1441–1493)*
Courtesy of the Uffizi Gallery, Florence
Photo: Scala/Art Resource, NY

Page 50, A DWARF AS A TURKISH PASHA *(1745–50), Italian porcelain (h. 6")*
Courtesy of the Metropolitan Museum of Art; The Jack & Belle Linsky Collection, 1982 (1982.60.368)

Page 54, *Parade sallet in the form of a lion's head (ca. 1460), Italian armor, steel and bronze, gilded and partly silvered with semiprecious stones (h. 11 1/8")*
Courtesy of the Metropolitan Museum of Art; Harris Brisbane Dick Fund, 1923 (23.141)

Page 56, *Equestrian Statue of Louis XIV by Gianlorenzo Bernini (1598–1680)*
    Courtesy of the Galleria Borghese, Rome
        Photo: Scala/Art Resource, NY

Page 57, DEPARTURE OF THE GREEK FLEET, *detail from mural by Giovanni Battista Tiepolo (1696–1770)*
    Courtesy of Villa Valmarana, Venice
        Photo: Art Resource, NY

Page 59, DAVID, *detail of marble statue by Michelangelo (1475–1564) (h. 13' 5")*
    Courtesy of the Academy, Florence
        Photo: Art Resource, NY

Page 63, ARTISAN *(late 1st century B.C.), Greek bronze (h. 16 15/16")*
    Courtesy of the Metropolitan Museum of Art; Rogers Fund, 1972 (1972.11.1)

Page 66, THE GREAT WILLOW AT GIVERNY *by Claude Monet (1840–1926), oil on canvas*
    Courtesy of a private collection, Geneva
        Photo: Giraudon/Art Resource, NY

Page 68, ALLIGATOR *(1975/88) by Earl Staley, acrylic on canvas (60 1/2 × 145")*
    Courtesy of the artist

Page 70, HERCULES SLAYING THE HYDRA *(ca. 1515), Majolica ware plate (diameter 14 1/2")*
    Courtesy of the Metropolitan Museum of Art; Robert Lehman Collection, 1975 (1975.1.1038)

Page 72, THE SECOND LABOUR OF HERCULES: THE LERNAEAN HYDRA *(1983) by Earl Staley, acrylic on canvas (64 × 48")*
    Courtesy of William and Virginia Camfield, Houston

BOOKS BY BERNARD EVSLIN

Merchants of Venus
Heroes, Gods and Monsters of the Greek Myths
Greeks Bearing Gifts: The Epics of Achilles and Ulysses
The Dolphin Rider
Gods, Demigods and Demons
The Green Hero
Heraclea
Signs & Wonders: Tales of the Old Testament